The River Twice

Princeton Series of Contemporary Poets
Susan Stewart, series editor

For other titles in the Princeton Series of Contemporary Poets see page 99

The River Twice

Poems

Kathleen Graber

PRINCETON UNIVERSITY PRESS
Princeton & Oxford

Requests for permission to reproduce material from this work should be sent to permissions@press.princeton.edu

Published by Princeton University Press
41 William Street, Princeton, New Jersey 08540
6 Oxford Street, Woodstock, Oxfordshire OX20 1TR

press.princeton.edu

Library of Congress Control Number: 2018965562
ISBN: 9780691193205
ISBN (pbk.): 9780691193212

British Library Cataloging-in-Publication Data is available

Editorial: Anne Savarese and Thalia Leaf
Production Editorial: Ellen Foos
Text and Jacket Design: Pamela Lewis Schnitter
Jacket/Cover Credit: Cover art paintings by Claudia de Vilafames courtesy of ArtDog London
Production: Merli Guerra
Publicity: Jodi Price and Keira Andrews
Copyeditor: Jodi Beder

This book has been composed in Adobe Garamond Pro and Scala Sans

Printed on acid-free paper. ∞

Printed in the United States of America

10 9 8 7 6 5 4 3 2 1

FOR SANDY TARANT

Wisdom is one thing—to know the intelligence by which all things are steered through all things; it is unwilling and yet willing to be called by the name of Zeus.

—Heraclitus

You cannot step twice into the same river, for other waters are continually flowing on.

—Heraclitus

Contents

ONE

Self-Portrait with No Internal Navigation

Have you ever been arrested? The pigeon arrests me.
No, not the wing but the sturdy round body & the sheen
of the throat, like the interior of a snail's shell or the bruise
of spring—think of the lilac blistered with blossoms,
of a burned moor's sudden eruption into heather—
a beauty we expect only from what's broken. Have you ever
gone too far? Last week, I overshot the same junction twice
along a simple stretch of country road. And Philippe Petit
crossed eight times between the Towers. Or this is what
the officers at the station told him later when he was through.
He had no idea how long he'd hovered, how many times
he had reversed himself, passing onto something almost
like earth beyond the far guy-wire, only to pivot back again—
lying down even, one leg dangling—above loose, swaying
space. I worry about the pigeons beginning today to roost
on the ferry that shuttles back & forth between two capes.
A pair of pigeons mates for a lifetime, produces, at most,
two squabs each year. They have chosen this spot because
centuries ago they were domestic—the words are *coop*
& *columbarium*—because they still love, past reason,
the swift tides of our voices, are drawn to the chattering
crew, even as it swats at them now with brooms & paints
the sooty pipes above the car deck with a chemical tar
concocted to burn the birds' feet. Once my husband stepped
out into open air. He fell but was somehow returned to me.
Feral cousin of the carrier & racer, the rock dove steers
with a certainty we cannot imagine. Still, what if one flies
into the marsh for reeds for the nest just as the boat sets sail?
How will it know to simply sit & wait? And what of the panic
of the one departed? The one who has left without leaving.

"The Weight"

"He did so many films on the impossibility of sainthood," says
Robertson about Buñuel, "people trying to be good in *Viridiana* and
Nazarin, people trying to do this thing. In 'The Weight' it's the same
thing. People like Bunuel would make films that had these religious
connotations to them but it wasn't necessarily a religious meaning."

—Robbie Robertson, quoted by Rob Bowman

Last night, when I closed the book, I was exactly forty-six pages
into a Norwegian novel thirty-six hundred pages long. The narrator
& his father are just sitting down to eat in silence a dinner

of pan-fried chops. It must have taken a kind of faith
to have composed this, as it will be an act of devotion to read it through
to the end.
                     My acupuncturist says it is not necessary to believe

in acupuncture for the needles to work. Lord, may there be a metaphor
here for all of the mysteries.
                          Each day I walk a line between my belief
in the sacred & my disbelief in the divine. Pins in my hands & arms,

toes & feet, my forehead, sometimes one pin in my chest. Once
he cured a head cold with two pins in my knee. Sometimes we talk
about Oregon or Austin, Colorado, the kidneys, the Beats. The liver,

The Byrd Theater on Cary Street, the restored pipe organ inside.

The bowel, the suboccipital triangle at the base of the skull. He says
he is trying to send more blood to my heart. Then he turns out the lights

& leaves me alone on the table, and I listen to the traffic on Thompson
shush by—
           old sound banking along a synapse to the room
behind the office
              where I slept those years my parents owned

The Off-Shore Motel: the tires, late on summer nights, still spinning
past toward the beach, the headlights through the window sweeping
the walls with light.
                 At a yard sale on Saturday, a girl wanted to buy

an old suitcase, but her mother wouldn't let her. *Maybe we could use
bleach*, the woman said, *but who knows what germs are lurking inside.*

Yet when I looked, it seemed nearly spotless—the little pouch

at the back held only one small pencil, the kind someone might use
to score a round of miniature golf. Sometimes at bedtime, my father
would sing to me—"Swinging on a Star," my favorite song,

though it would have been an oldie even then.
                                    I rarely think
of any of this, just as I don't think of my father existing anywhere
anymore, other than inside the heads of the few of us left who can still

recall him. He gambled away almost all the money he ever made.

Last week, a pilot intentionally flew a plane into the Alpine mountain
beside which he had glided as a boy.
                        The novelist says the only things

in a face that do not age are the eyes—the changes in our vision
presumably invisible to the person looking in.
                                 When the acupuncturist
returns, he takes my hand in his small hand. He touches the tips

of his fingers to my fingers to see if they have warmed.
                                          Lord,
these days it is as though I am returned again at every moment
from so far away. The worn palm of the world is heavy with time.

America [peaches]

America, I know I could do better by you,
though I stoop conscientiously three times a day
to pick up my dog's waste from the grass
with black biodegradable bags. And lest you suspect
that this is more pretension than allegiance, know
my dog was the one at the shelter no one else
would take. He is fat & lazy & I could do better
by him as well, though I do not know if a long walk
in the park in ninety-seven-degree heat is a good idea.
Please cue a presidential sound bite to reassure me
all hearts are more resilient than I think. I confess
it would have been a moral error to have embraced him
if I did not have the means to keep him fed. But
I am writing tonight because there is something wrong
with your peaches. The ones from the supermarket
are so soft & cheap—half the cost of the ones
sold at the local farm—but the flesh near the pit
is so bitter & green. It is a fruit like the mind
we are making together: both overripe & immature.
Trust me, I still have the simple tastes you gave me:
I am delighted by the common robins & cardinals,
the way they set the trees at dusk aflame. Thank you
for Tuesday's reliable trash collection. If you are
constellated somehow, a little bit inside
each of your people, I am sorry that there is more
& more of you lately I do not understand.
Sometimes I want simply to sit alone a long time
in silence. America, you must want this too.

Self-Portrait with *The Sleeping Man*

—after the photograph by Markéta Luskačová

1.

Sometimes when I cannot sleep, I conjure the famous photograph
of the Slovakian peasant sleeping by the side of the road
in order to put my own disquiet in perspective.

                                        What is my restlessness

beside his need? Or I think of my own foreign body origami-ed
into its blue seat on a plane—the flight long, one-way, intergalactic—
or my body huddled against the gray window of a bus or a train

as it pushes across another state line. Sometimes, then, I remember
the year we lost everything, the years I lived in an illegal attic apartment
without a stove.

                    Last week, my brother's wife's brother—

alcoholic for decades—fell down a flight of steps in the dark
& has not been able to move his limbs since.

                                        Having been abandoned
by his wife, he had to send his four-year-old daughter

through the woods at dawn to ask a neighbor for help. The child
has never lived close enough to a town to have played with other children.
She stutters & cries.

                    Her name is the name we call out when someone asks

for the name of a terrible storm—one in which people cling to their roofs
& beg to be saved.

                    Some things we only think we can imagine.

Once a scholar was in love with the word *recognition,* the word *shock.*

Sometimes I can barely recognize my own upended life. Each morning,
I wake with no idea of where I am, no longer with even the expectation
of knowing.

Last night, I dreamt I was climbing a steep hill in cold daylight.

My dog was climbing beside me. My only fear was the fear he would slip.

Perhaps every meaning is obvious & ancient. The day's news offers
again the relentless brutality of its sad, un-fake facts.

Let's be clear

about how dumb I still am:

Sometimes I say *I,* as though someone
might still believe there could be a coherent, distinct self in here.
Sometimes I forget that I cannot say *I,* or I assume that you know that

when I say *I,* I mean *we.* Or that I at least want to mean *we,* even when
grammar or the simple ethics of the situation seems to demand *you* or,
worse yet, *them.*

As in today: Two women—blood on their faces & hands,

their scarves—stepping arm-in-arm, over the bodies fallen around them,
after cars painted to look like ambulances explode on a street.

2.

He seems to slumber so soundly there—though he must have worries

& pain, exhaustion—out in the open, in a coarse suit, heavy socks,
his thin frame folded into the mossy roots of a tree, his palm cupping
his skull, to make a kind of pillow,

the way my father used to sleep.

Pilgrims, both of them now past stirring,

their last dreams already dreamt.

Caught in the 1960s by a Czech photographer, the sleeper seems
beyond time, as though he has crossed a border from another realm,

from a time
            out of which only memories can be smuggled,
like round blue boxes of salt. Think of all the ordinary days
for which no camera had yet been invented.
                                Right now, I am trying

to look hard at the shoulders
                        & curved beak of a hawk
perched on a bare branch as it scans the lawn waiting for something
small to move.
                I have not forgotten the cold days I paid for beans

& apples with a fist of copper coins.
                                Another way to be *awakened*.
And though I have never slept in a doorway—or rather only once,
in Paris, when I was just nineteen—
                        now I cannot not see the places

I could, if I ever had to, put myself down to rest.
                                The hawk
has vision eight times sharper than our own. It can detect a flicker,
a pulse. It will live for twenty years this way in the wild.
                                Yet perhaps

vigilance & hunger, perhaps even terror, have their bounds.
                                At dusk
the hawk rotates its neck 180 degrees & rests its head on its own back
as it sleeps. It fluffs its feathers, tucks its fierce eyes beneath its wing.

America [flight]

Even scientists are baffled by how Holly, a 4-year-old tortoiseshell who in early November became separated from Jacob and Bonnie Richter at an R.V. rally in Daytona Beach, Fla., appeared on New Year's Eve—staggering, weak and emaciated—in a backyard about a mile from the Richters' house in West Palm Beach.

—Pam Belluck, *New York Times*

America, I have a friend for whom everything went south
after the death of her cat. It seems melodramatic
& hyperbolic to say so, though sometimes
even the melodramatic & hyperbolic are true. Another truth:
She saw it coming, but there was nothing she could do.
First, she adopted two feral kittens someone had found
in a garage, & when that didn't work, she phoned
the local shelter & took in five more. Like the everything
that unfolded thereafter, the opening act was slower
& more complicated than I am making it now. Today,
I drove a long way to the airport in order to fly directly
into a blizzard & back. Someone in a control tower
somewhere should have known this was a bad idea—
something we all wake up early in order to discover
we don't actually have to do. But there was no red alert
from the airline in the inbox above the forwarded story
of a tortoiseshell cat in Florida which had found its way
two hundred miles home. America, because we would like
to know where we are going & what we will find,
scientists have released animals inside planetariums
& tied magnets to the heads of turtles in order to prove
that it is possible to set them off course. They have
surgically removed most of the anatomy from living

homing pigeons & still, we are stuck with the words
instinct & *gut.* Also sometimes *amazing aptitude.*
Holly was reduced to skin & bones & raw footpads.

Domestic cats rarely pass through the Everglades alive.
Do not be ashamed. Who doesn't have a hungry wilderness
inside? On the plane, I sat between a Jehovah's Witness
& a student of cognitive psychology on his way to a job
at a memory lab. She read aloud her favorite passages
about love & judgment. She said, *The Lord gave us a chance*
to be gardeners and look what we've done. America,
we know seabirds only fly on starry nights & the dung beetle
pushes its golden ball in a perfectly straight line, using
the Milky Way as its guide. Sometimes I try to forget
where I am. Who would not feel frightened on a burning
planet? In a radioactive sea? It's not faith or loyalty. Only fact.
We are small & afield. Give me your hand in the dark.

New Year

New measurements by the European Space Agency's Planck satellite—
which studied the cosmic microwave background, or the light left over
from the Big Bang—indicate that this period of light began about
100 million years later than Planck's previous estimate. "While these
100 million years may seem negligible compared to the universe's age
of almost 14 billion years, they make a significant difference when
it comes to the formation of the first stars," Marco Bersanelli of the
University of Milan, and a member of the Planck Collaboration, said
in a statement.

—Calla Cofield, *Space.com*

The most brilliant comet was Donati's, which last appeared in 1858.
No one alive now will ever see it, as astronomers calculate the duration

of its elliptical orbit to be nineteen hundred years. My older brother
never lived to see the cell phone. When he died, my portable computer

weighed fourteen pounds.
                          Some truths are ugly:
The New World Black Vulture, for instance, is a threat to farmers

& ranchers; a gang, working together, will sometimes take down
a newborn calf or a lamb—ripping at the animal's face & eyes

until it passes into shock, then devouring it alive. A bird: half predator,
half pure pathway from flesh to flight.

                          Today, like all days,

is another beginning. Nearly warm. And the vultures untuck
their heads, spread their wings & hold, hold, hold.

                          Salutation:

forty perched in the crowded limbs above me. But when I say aloud,
They are all gone now, they do not move.

                          Who knows the dead

better than they do?
                    Sometimes I stand in the road to watch them
elegantly angling home. The sky, a busy runway, as the shadows

of the oaks—
                    their branches like charts of the body's systems—
define themselves on the hard dirt.
                              Today we say *finally*

& *again*. We say *resolution*. Some birds already circle above
the fields, but most merely pose, bathing in the sun, waiting for the air

to warm & rise into the thermals on which they glide. And because
they have no vocal organs, the stand of trees where they loaf

gives off only an electric hiss & hum.
                              Their name in Latin
means *tearer* or *purifier*. Cathartidae, as in *catharsis*. Clothed in black.

Birdwatchers call the white feathers at the tips of their wings *stars*.
Far off, the glossy crows scream. Nearby, the chickadee & the thrush.

Only me, the dog, & a young girl, jogging, her earbuds erasing
the world's low winter song. Soon, the owl behind the house, maybe

a mouse in the kitchen.
                    The Tibetans & the Mayans knew the vulture
is both practical & holy.
                    In one creation myth, it is the Earth's mason,

lime plastering the front of its apron, as digestion turns the forsaken
into splashes of immaculate light.
                              Once there were two photographs

of Donati's comet—the first comet ever caught on film—one taken
by a Harvard astronomer, the other—supposedly far better, but lost—

by an unheard-of photographer in England with only his portrait lens.
Yesterday, a friend called to ask how long I think our grief continues.

He's lost his gloves, the last gift his wife will ever give him.
And though I said *Forever,* I meant, of course, something less.

The Year of the Horse

No longer the thought that you *have* a body, but, rather,
that you *are* one. Only yesterday, a student, long-haired,
not yet twenty, asked if this were even a distinction
that made any sense. It's late already in a neighborhood
so suburban all the drivers wave as they pass
though no one knows anyone's name. The streets
so quiet that even the house rented to kids
from the pricey private college has gone sleepily dark.
The last image you have of home is of an injured gull
shrieking amid the traffic of the 7-Eleven parking lot.
A man with a baseball cap trying to shoo it off,
but it won't fly. You thought that if a car didn't
crush it soon, the guy at the gas pumps might finally—
out of compassion rather than cruelty—walk over
on his break & crush its head with a boot. Its suffering
seemed that relentless. The night before, a full moon
had pulled the tide so high turtles were left stranded
in the road beside the marshes, but, here, now, is
an evening so capacious no one needs a scarf or gloves.
No one has to decide. Decades ago, if you passed
among illuminated brownstones, you wondered how
you had missed some turn of fate that might have
given you the keys. Not yet knowing the days
when you won't eat or dress, not yet the Year of the Ox
when you'll have only debt. Inside, on the stove,
chicken, carrots, parsley, & dill. Broth as transparent
as habit. As for sorrow: in other states, the mothers
& fathers of everyone you love are dying, but yours
are already dead. Some things only happen once. Above,
the perfectly credible stars. Below, a downhill road.
Last week's snow melting before the next storm arrives.

TWO

Beginner's Mind

Because, for Suzuki, the sufficient mind is not *closed*, but *empty & ready*,
I am diligently preparing—

            my computer hypnotically streaming

episode after episode of *My So-Called Life* on demand.

                                This morning,
when I hit the button on the car radio, Neil Young poured out—

Hey hey, my my—& I felt as conflicted as an adolescent. The message
of the lyrics irresistible, of course, & wrong. But, soon, there was only

the endless loop of a jumbo jet over the South China Sea—

                                    in an instant,
offline & gone.

                Hour after hour of nothing-more-to-report, punctuated

by Russia in Crimea & an interview with Jared Leto, an Academy Award
in his palm.

               Isn't the dream of all technology to trace the history of the stars

back to their start?

               The plot is a constellation of inarticulate angst
& charm: his portrayal of teenage opacity perfectly clear.

                                      This is called

Emptiness, Suzuki writes. *We should always live*, he tells us, *in the dark
empty sky.*

               And so, I would like a panel of experts to discuss

the magnetically beautiful & silent

                               because I cannot keep the bats out
of the house. Because I live so near the marshes, because the building

is unusually high.
They—who can wing cleanly through a tight grid
of fine wire—somehow still manage to bumble their way in. Often only

to glide out again—inaudible shadow—through an open window,
though once—perhaps already ill—one crawled into a rubber rain boot

in the hall closet to die in the dark.
Maybe this is why we cannot stop
studying the heavens, its cry, like the bat's, a beacon passing through us

at a frequency two octaves too high.
Given the night's velvet, our dream
is of what we cannot see, some evermore astonishing depth beyond.

Imagine a whole season of Bill Murray whispering into the ear
of Scarlett Johansson words just beyond our ability to hear.

Already I suspect we will never understand.
My dread & sorrow
are only the same ineffable dread & sorrow everyone must feel.

Before dawn, the birds in the leafless branches plug in their amplifiers
& turn it up. And now, into the evening, the red-bellied woodpecker

hammers on & on. We would like to live like the finch or the fish,
yet we are, at best, the *worst kind of horse.*
The series finale

couldn't be more ambiguous, production canceled just as the conflict
has finally begun.
But there—whenever you want to find it—

is the scene in which Jared Leto takes for the first time the manic hand
of Claire Danes in his own in the high school hallway.

He says, *Can we go somewhere?* And when she says, *Sure,* they do.

America [train]

America, by the time I got to the box elder, the cricket
was already dead. I had found it in the closet, chirping
between two shoes, & trapped it in a tumbler, holding a postcard
across the rim. But its legs were too strong, or its fear,
&, in a matter of moments, it destroyed itself, propelling itself
again & again against the glass. Let us tell ourselves
it was merely stunned by the collision, that it revived later,
coming to as a sparrow might, exactly where I left it
in the grass. Let me say I was merely trying to do the right thing.
I keep thinking of the Chinese proverb: *You have to catch
your own luck.* Last week in Longmont, Colorado,
just down the street from where my brother lives, a girl—
eighteen, a college freshman—lost both her legs trying to catch
a freight train with two friends just for kicks. And I think
of my uncle, hungry, broke, hopping across the early thirties
until he could land a job with my father, working
the custodial nightshift at Greystone, mopping floors
as the mad, insomniac women pounded their heads
against the bars. Three economic analysts report the dawn
of a new reality. America, neither I nor any of this exists:
There is only *the Plutonomy.* And *the rest* is merely, as they say,
the rest. And yet the tracks still run beside the white monumental
chicken-processing plant at the end of Main Street—
it's an old redbrick cowboy town—& the train slows right there
as it intersects the road. I've sat mesmerized—O, the immensity
of the West—in a rental car at the crossing, watching it pass
& pass. I don't remember ever thinking I was invincible—
though I must have thought you were—though we say now
that that's what all kids think. You are our world-
body, you, who taught us each thing wants only to be more.

Bitter Vetch

> Oxen are happy when they find bitter vetches to eat.
>
> —Heraclitus

Because my landlord's ex-lover has just moved
into the unheated, unfinished basement, there is so much
now I'd like to say, whereas I can only cook—two floors up,
in the attic apartment—brown lentils & steamed broccoli
on a two-burner hot plate. I put one marinated salmon fillet
into a forty-year-old Kenmore countertop oven that runs
on a timer & pings a tinny ping when it's done. How luxurious,
though, in middle age to have a roof & radiators, enough
hot water & a tub for a bath. One restless year, I thought
at night instead of dreaming of the monster huddled
in the freezing sty & of the crack in the wall through which
he studied words & firelight & the face of a blind man
so long he believed the world was as harmless & flush
as an immense, undulating cirrus bank illuminated
by January sun. Maybe I'm misremembering that story
& maybe it's shameful to say it gave me strange comfort
to think of him & maybe Mary Shelley poured into her book
a crystallized rage, nearly ice, at a god who seemed
to have made us then left us all more than a bit in the dark.
For this is how it is to look through one thing in order to see
another. The first glass was, after all, obsidian, an opaque
matter not of our making, a substance fashioned in nature
by circumstance rather than design. Which must be how
the woman somewhere below me tonight, my age—
& on the surface, at least, perfectly normal—sees her life,

in the shape of a continent or a galloping horse, dispersing,
as she drifts above a sump pump & a French drain
on a narrow camp cot beside someone else's washer & dryer,
buried from chin to toes beneath a borrowed electric throw.

The Zeitgeist Bird

. . . like a huge wet bird on a branch, suddenly and without a clear
reason unexpectedly takes off in bold and joyous flight. We all hear
the shush of this flight. It stirs our imagination and gives us energy;
we begin to act.

—Ryszard Kapuściński

Stopped at the light behind license plate XNG 1066,
I think, as anyone would, of the Battle of Hastings
& what descendant of William or impassioned historian
is driving a battered Sentra through the new millennium
up Broad Street in Richmond, Virginia. But, of course,
it's likely this message has got less to do with genetics
& a Norman fleet's floating on felled trees across
the English Channel than the random generation of letters
& digits by a central processing unit at the DMV.

And I feel afraid, for a moment, for my mind that whirled
so excitedly around a code that wasn't there. Which is
to say, the bird is not there, has not been there, is extinct,
if it ever was. Kapuściński's great zeitgeist bird
we think we hear some mornings lifting off, as if stirred
by the whistle of cosmic winds to direct us into the next
great age, which I say now, without any evidence,
will be less ironic than the last. Which is to say, we direct
ourselves though no one is directing, less like those
geese in a V going south & north & south again
behind their stalwart rotating front men than like a ball
of roosting blackbirds sent careening by a car alarm
at dusk from Shafer Street's two dozen Bradford Pears.

And when they fall from the sky somewhere in Arkansas
by the thousands, their breasts exploded from having
apparently flown into the brittle fortress of themselves,
an expert will materialize to assure us that even this
is no cause for concern, even this is far more common
than anyone would think. Psychologists call it *apophenia,*
an abundance of meaning, the symptom of finding
in everything the message everything lacks.

In 1842, after carefully recording every empty pinhole
in the Bayeux Tapestry, someone set out with a needle
& wool to restore it—& more or less did—
so that now, here still, we can find King Harold's men,
shoulder to shoulder in tactical shield-wall formation:
the spears in their right hands raised already
above their heads, while in their lefts, they cradle
to their armored chests their brilliant blue & gold wings.

Labyrinth

Sometimes the sides of the fishing boats in the canal were red & the wheel-houses were white. Or the sides were white & the wheelhouses blue. There were nets & bails, winches. Smokestacks & pale wooden crates. I would load six books into my backpack: three I had read & would read again & three I had never read before. Can we call this risk? Heading out on my brother's orange Schwinn—my feet barely touching the pedals—to sit on the dock going nowhere. To set sail is such a dangerous business. Last night, when a woman reminded us that we might yet be better together than we are apart, I felt as buoyant as I had a month ago when three Tarot cards revealed their unambiguous good news. If we are taking on water, it is, for now, only the metaphoric kind, meaning something else broken in the house we don't have the money to fix. The compressor roars, but the temperature will not come down. Once I fell asleep on the bus to the city & woke to find the man seated beside me holding my hand. I was too young to know enough to be frightened. Later, he took a bag of pills from his pocket & offered me as many as I'd like. In the distance, there was al-ready the profile of a bridge. Here, in the great heat of the day, a legless man rolls his wheelchair along the highway: a small gray dog, on a rope leash, trots along beside him. We call what contained the Minotaur a laby-rinth, but it was a maze. A labyrinth is its own thread. The longest suspen-sion bridge is in Kobe, Japan. The second longest is in China. I am wind-ing away from who I was, looking far across at someone studying her painted toes & sandals, a self looking across at another self, singing low & off-key, *Baby, I wanna go home.* There is only one way forward. Once upon a time, everyone had a different life. The pier cast down a deep lavender shadow, turned the water green in the narrow harbor.

America [October]

America, some days I can barely read the postcards
I have been getting each week from a friend, broken
loose & adrift for months along your back roads & highways.
Pictures of mountains & monuments, postmarked,
but with no return address: West Virginia, Nashville,
Oklahoma, Deadwood, South Dakota. So that, like you,
my mailbox has become merely the idea of *listening*
into which he speaks but out of which I offer
no reply. Just as most of us would have nothing to say
to the scientists at CERN who announced this week
that the universe should not exist, for even after
extraordinary study, they do not know why matter
& antimatter, so perfectly balanced, did not cancel
one another out at the start. So, instead, here we are,
late October: a few petunias hanging on in their planters,
leaves beginning to cover the lawns. Everywhere this
atmosphere of abundant powerlessness & apprehension.
Each thought, a tiny house loaded floor to ceiling.
Each word, a packed box. I think of a small boy alone
in his own garage, hiding there because his dad has left
the family & he is too sad to go to school. Maybe
he walks over to the tidy crate of ornaments & tinsel
that once belonged to his grandmother, maybe
he puts his foot inside the red & green tree stand
as though it were a shoe. By the door, the folded
beach umbrella is still dusted with sand. Somewhere,
there is a felt elephant with a torn ear, a little blue hat.

Across the river is a statue of Robert E. Lee
no one ever meant to be invisible. America,

are you the mute hypochondriac whose cold solace
will be the mantra *I told you I was sick,* though
no one would have heard you say it? You were
conceived in a genocidal, colonial violence,
& yet, like the universe, you & I are here today,
going on & on, discovering that we were naïve,
or simply wrong, about almost everything we thought
we knew. *Truth*, an envelope with nothing inside.

The boy, however, feels filled with his anger & shame
at not being able to imagine how to make things right.
Maybe his teacher is writing on the board the word
constitution. Or the word *cumulous.* Maybe the class
is watching a video about clouds or the Liberty Bell.
The world is full of little boys who could tell this boy
that he doesn't know the first thing about suffering. And,
of course, they would be right. And they would be wrong.
What good is a theory of relative trauma to him? Still,
his father isn't threatening, after all, to become merely
the idea of father or the memory of father, or worse,
the hollow place where the memory or idea of father
might have been. His father has moved into a condo
one town over; he still coaches his son's soccer team.

Outside, morning is announcing its shy singularity,
another day dyed in stunning, unoriginal light.
The view from the porch is the view from the porch.
And yet, we are older. America, how do we feel
as we hover again under the lintel, caught between
stoic resolve & some impulse toward wild action?
Here, the squirrels—what could be more mundane?—
dart & stop, dart & stop. One holds up, as if
it were an unborn cosmos, a green pignut in its paws.

Impasto for the Parietal

> Alone in that vastness, lit by the feeble beam of our lamps,
> we were seized by a strange feeling. . . . Time was abolished,
> as if the tens of thousands of years that separated us from
> the producers of these paintings no longer existed.
>
> —Jean-Marie Chauvet et al.

1

After the anthropology students discovered the cave in Ardèche,
they told the interviewer that they had felt *like intruders*. They said

they could feel the presence of the other souls around them. *Everything
was so beautiful, so fresh. . . .*

                  My mother used to say that it was too easy

to forget the beauty of the place we lived.

                        And so, lately, I have been trying
to discover the sea by walking into the sea—

                    in the evening, after work,

after the lifeguards have all called it a day. I rarely go deeper
than my waist or my chest, though when I was younger, I would push out

past the breakers to float a long time on my back at dusk. And once,
in the late fall, when my retriever bolted so far into the surf

he seemed only another bobbing dot of foam, I pulled off my shoes & socks
& swam out above my head to haul him back.

                      I don't know what I am doing
there now alone these days.

                I stare into the immensity, half-thinking
I am executing some moral obligation to stand on the Earth

as consciously as I can for as long as I am able.

                  Or I think of the horizons
Hiroshi Sugimoto captured on film. The photographer says that every time

he views the sea he feels as if he is visiting the home of his ancestors.
No matter how cold the water, I make myself dive again & again.

Today I overheard a young woman outside the library talking
on her phone. *When I told my grandmother that I hate him now, she said,*

oh, honey, you're a fool 'cause that's just some other kind of love.
Perhaps this is as close as most of us will ever come to the oracular.

I have rarely known with any real depth or precision what it is I felt.

2

Sometimes, late at night, I read the hypotheses:

the possible meanings

of the Paleolithic art.

Or I reread the old essays of Loren Eiseley,
who proposed all life might be a backward yearning toward the dark.

There were the mammals, he writes, after all, *who had given up the land
and returned to the sea . . .*

fish that slept in the mud, birds that no longer flew.

His is an *apologia,* equal parts ode & elegy, praise for what we might call
a fierce curiosity & a lamentation for his boyhood friend, *The Rat,*

who used to guide their gang through the labyrinth of the city's sewers—
before he died, at ten, from an illness which today might easily be cured.

Saussure thought every story was a story in which all the meanings lie
between,

yet Freud believed there were subterranean passages, a world

of desires that always remains closed, even to ourselves.
The question for scholars has never been why paint, but why paint

in a place so hidden.

Of course, this is no longer a riddle
anyone who will ever live will ever solve, though, even across 35,000 years,

it still seems to me incomprehensible

that the secret has been lost.
Didn't someone always tell someone to always tell someone to pass it on?

3

In high school, I liked to walk along the shore & dream about the boy
who sat in front of me in math class. How he wore his sun-bleached hair

in a ponytail & how he could solve the most difficult calculus equations
at the board without effort, even though he'd just been outside at lunch

with his friends getting stoned.
                              The only living things in sight
were the little sandpipers & the black-headed laughing gulls,

though the wrack line glittered with flotsam: waxy garlands
we called sea snakes—whose pouches contained hundreds of tiny whelks—

& the cracked armature of the prehistoric horseshoe crabs, barnacles
fastened to their burnished backs & tails.
                                      Maybe it is because I wanted

so much to be fathomed—as far as it is possible for a teenager to be—
that he would never come near.
                              He grew up to be a sixth-grade teacher,

& a co-worker found him dead on his kitchen floor one day
in December after he failed to show up to his class.
                                              I try to tell myself

none of this could have been any better than it was: the merely
imagined, some uncontainable churn, always richer than the known.

Or, to say it another way:
                        longing, too, is three parts salt—

4

Sometimes I open a book of color plates & trace with my finger

the curled bison sleeping on the ceiling at Altamira & the one
delicately drawn deer nearby.

Wrapped in silence, they only become

even more of whatever it is they already are:

urgent & archetypal,
whether their images were meant to be a kind of magic or prayer

or not.

I have a friend who says she has sometimes felt time *collapse*—
the diachronic & the synchronic—

but this has never happened for me.

The furthest-back thing I can recall is my grandmother's shoe—
sturdy, open-toed, with laces. She lived in the green & white trailer

behind our house, & each morning, I sipped coffee with milk & sugar
from her saucer before she buttoned my coat & walked us to church—

our parish named for St. Anne, the mother of the mother of God.
She folded her hands. I folded mine.

Regarding the heart, I wanted

to offer you a wilder, bolder being—but there is still only this
mind in the cave, earthbound & self-aware, though, even now,

the late sun washes, as it always has, the waves with its red light.

THREE

The River Twice

The Love of Jesus is a thrift warehouse on the south side of town. Everything

inside is a dollar. On Mondays & Fridays, everything is fifty cents.
A stormy afternoon in June & I drift for hours down the aisles: bread machines

& coffee pots. Shirts
                      & shoes. Teetering stacks of mismatched dinnerware.

I am studying a cup whose crackled glaze is the pale blue-green
of beach glass. Two lions chase one another around its fragile eternity

the way the lover pursues the beloved on the ancient urn, their manes & legs

washed in a preternatural purple & gold.
                         Behind me, a woman tells her son
William to get up from the floor so that she can measure him against a pair

of little boys' jeans. When he doesn't rise, she tells him she is going to start

counting. She says she is only going to count to two.
                         When I look over,
he is already on his feet at silent attention, his arms outstretched from his sides.

I live in an attic apartment above two women who have been unemployed

as long as I have known them.
                    This week the last of their benefits
have been unexpectedly terminated by the state.
                        A drop in the overall number

of jobless automatically triggers the cessation of extensions, the letters

that come in the mail explain.
                    Outside, thunder cracks. Later, the streets
will be full of limbs.
                Heraclitus believed that in the beginning

35

creation simply bubbled forth, an inevitable percolating stream—*logos,*

both reason & word—issuing from a source unseen. Sometimes
I feel a sudden sorrow, as though my own emotions were a room

I'd forgotten why I entered.
                                My mother struck me only once—

for refusing to put on my coat. I was four years old & she had been scrubbing
motel rooms all day.
                        I'd fallen asleep in the dark on a low shelf

in the linen closet beside the boxes of little pink soaps.
                                                Today, that shelf

is gone & the great white polar caps
                                    are melting. At Kasungu National Park
in Malawi, a drought has caused the lions to turn on the rangers

whose job it is to protect them.
                            Our skulls are chipped bowls, broken

globes, we plunge into the flow.
                            Heraclitus, whom the crash of time has left
in fragments, saw in the cosmos a harmony of tensions.
                                                Imagine

the lyre, he wrote, & the bow. The store radio plays satellite gospel.

A hymn with the chorus *Every moment you shall be judged* is followed
by one in which the choir shouts *Praise! Stand up and be forgiven.*

America [superstorm]

America, I would like to get closer to you, but
you are the unconscious patient. One hundred interns
bicker this morning above your bed. Yesterday,
I read for no reason an essay written a decade ago
on game theory & economics. Apparently, the problem
with accurate predictions is that sometimes people
simply don't make the rational choice. Illness & sleep
are weary metaphors. The poor, who are now homeless—
displaced by a storm—rest their heads tonight
in luxury beachfront hotel rooms. *All I want,*
one woman says, *is my old kitchen where I could cook*
a hot meal for my kids. Soon a young man will walk
into a classroom of six-year-olds & empty his gun.
The problem with life is that everyone who dies
really dies. In Belgium, twin brothers petition
to be euthanized. Born deaf, they are losing their vision.
Trained as shoemakers, they have spent every day
side by side. Another sibling says they have battled
pain all of their lives. They say they cannot imagine
being able to know one another only by touch.
When my brother was failing, his wife roamed the ward
wild-eyed & inconsolable. *It's not what it seems,*
she whispered when she thought no one could hear.
His cells are regenerating. Tomorrow he'll open
his eyes and be fine. The day he died a surgeon
offered to install a system of shunts that would not
have saved him. They would, however, have drained
the fluid collecting around his heart. My brother
had left papers that said I should be the decider.

America, sometimes all options are poor options.
He died before anything more could happen.
That is all I remember. I have no idea what I said.

Landscape with No One in It

The woman thinks she can hear the train whistle more clearly & more often because the leaves are gone or because the air is colder, though she knows sound travels more slowly as the temperature falls. Maybe the years were like that: racing by in their heat at a rate that made them inaudible. But speed is immaterial now, for folding the towels, stitching a hem, or scrubbing the pots with a honed efficiency only seems to multiply the minutes of the predawn morning she is trying to fill—activities as point-less & repetitive as spooning sand with a tiny shovel into a battered colan-der, as she had done at the beach when she was small. *It's not my job,* her husband had said on the way out, *to keep you from being lonely.* Last night she dreamt she was standing at the foot of a staircase. Above, she could hear someone playing "Autumn Leaves" on a piano. Climbing the steps to see, she found only an automated instrument—the keys moving, but no one there. All night, the same song, over & over. Again & again, finally, still, no one there. Now, dusting the picture frames, she thinks she would like someone to fall in love one day with the silly paint-by-number boat she'd bought at a yard sale, its titanium white sail full & its black hull & cadmium red deck leaning into the heavy monastral blue. Once a man had shown her how to right a *turtled* vessel. Even when it flips upright, he had explained, someone has to stay down, underwater—he'd even held his breath for a moment to make it clear—hugging the centerboard while someone else, topside, frantically works the ropes, drops the sails. Outside the wind is shaking loose the acorns & hazelnuts, brown shells pinging off the porch & the walk. Rolling the plastic can to the curb in pink light, she imagines she might be the only person left alive—surprised that the thought is not unbearable, surprised by how peculiarly her solitude has tuned her.

Greetings from Wildwood (or Thinking of James Wright & Everything Else in the World)

One afternoon—as I was bagging & boarding 300 hundred comic books
from the early '80s for resale in our boardwalk shop—a young man

told me, with utter earnestness, that he'd been looking a long time
for the right superhero.

     In fact, only recently had it occurred to him

that *You know, Daredevil really is a dude with a lot going on.* And
it's true: the Daredevil is smart—though blind—& like so many

of his kind, a mutant orphan, more or less.

       And though he often chooses
violence, he seems to at least halfway dislike it. He'd certainly rather not

take anyone's life.

    It isn't an exaggeration to say it meant a lot to us both
that I could understand where he stood on the subject, for it isn't easy

to recognize what counts.

     On my desk—beside the two unopened volumes
on practical ethics I bought last year—is a green plastic action figure

of the Swamp Thing, a hulking vegetable elemental, who has absorbed
the memory of a murdered scientist & therefore suffers from the delusion

of thinking he is a man.

    It has been years since a friend left a message
telling me her husband had just told her their eighteen-year marriage

was done. The reason, if even knowable, must have seemed to her then
both vitally important & nearly beside the point.

       When I scan a shelf,

I catch the blue cardstock edge of a stapled anthology that contains
a poem my younger brother wrote when he was twenty-one:

Though geese can fly, they cannot kiss in Philadelphia alleyways.

I cannot remember now the name of the girl for whom he wrote it.

He's been married so long to someone else.
                                        It is our mother's birthday.
She would be ninety, though she is not, so here, too, is a stack

of her worn books on competitive bridge: overcalls & preemptive bidding.

The Daredevil has been trying since 1964 to clean things up.

After the comic book fan left, a man my own age, or a little older,
came in with a sad story:
                        his hotel room had been robbed. He asked

if there was anything he could do—something he could clean
or repair perhaps—to earn a little money. He'd filed a police report,

but the officer had said there are so many thefts:
                                        the city would go broke
if they gave bus fare to everyone who asked.
                                        He looked scared & ashamed.

He said he'd spent hours on a bench in the sun trying to figure out a way
to get home.
            In the end, he claimed the cost of the journey would be

twelve dollars & change, & though I don't think I'm naïve or generous,
I handed it to him.
                    A few days later I would see him cruising a side street

on a battered bike & know I had been scammed, but he must have worked
hard concocting so compelling a plot.
                                    His performance, impeccable;

the details, just right.
                        He said he didn't know anyone able to help.
And maybe it mattered that I had once been alone in a foreign city

& just that poor myself.

For most philosophers, there is no virtue greater
than reason.

Aquinas is called an empiricist now because he believed

we could know the world as it is.

He thought we could even know
the unknown through the known, know God through His creation,

tracing back through everything that needs a cause to that which needs
none.

Tonight when I finally turn to the ethicist's great tomes, I will only feel

a little lonelier, imagining that we might be the only rational beings
in the universe.

There may be life elsewhere, he writes, *but there may be*

no other animals like us.

The Swamp Thing thinks that he is human.
I have sometimes wished to be something else.

His one job is to protect

the swamp, yet still, somehow, he manages to find a white-haired, telepathic
woman & fall in love. And when he does, the wild tubers sprouting

from the impossible landscape of his back

break into blossom, a blooming,
beyond figure & guile—its tender script evident, undeniable, bright.

America [Assateague]

America, *Every explorer names his island Formosa, beautiful.*
This is what Walker Percy tells us. For *being first*, he alone
has access to it and can see it for what it is. And every child calls
its imagined pony by its secret name, a word to summon a large
& gentle wildness from empty air, its long face & warm breath
visible in that moment before it touches its muzzle to the dreaming
brow. In one metaphor, America, the tips of your right hand
might be the Aleutians; those of your left, the Florida Keys.

Today, everyone has come to see the horses, who have been here
for four hundred years. In myth, they descend from a herd
brought on a Spanish galleon & swim ashore to their astonishing
freedom after the ship hits a sandbar in a storm & goes down.
America, this is a scene you have seen before: a dark hull of flesh.
Or they are the descendants of horses set out by farmers to graze
& inexplicably forgotten. You are an assemblage. Natural.
Unnatural. So little of you is not from somewhere else.

In the woods, where we cannot see them, the small spotted elk
from Taiwan—renamed *deer*, though their DNA would reveal
that that is not what they are—are settling down to sleep.
The sky & marsh purple & flood with the perfectly familiar:
the bat, the house mouse, the raccoon. The Norway rat & possum.
The least shrew. The meadow jumping mouse. The fox, the vole.

And birds: eagles, ospreys, egrets, merlins & mallards, pintails
& even the remarkable & invasive Canada geese. So that
if I were pulled from my bed in the night to identify your body,
I might look here, to this island—half-north, half-south—as one does
to the pale, beloved & often-fingered freckle on the cocked hip
of a lover—where, even in twilight, a band of feral horses stirs

in the cordgrass & briar. The light, alive in their dark eyes,
is an elegy to that species of shouting wonder emitted only
by toddlers before our wonder falls silent & reverential. *Animals,*
John Berger asserts, *first entered the imagination* not as leather
or meat but *as messengers and promises,* a lament, or an augury,
for our tongues, before both our desire & outrage became crude.

The Fifth Season

Metaphysics is the science of being as being. The concept of being is
the simplest of all concepts, and it is irreducible to other more ultimate
concepts: being, therefore, cannot be defined. We can conceive being
distinctly by itself, for in its widest significance it simply means
that which includes no contradiction, that which is not intrinsically
impossible; but every other concept, every concept of a distinct kind of
being, includes the concept of being.

—Frederick Copleston on John Duns Scotus

1.

I own almost nothing now that once belonged to my older brother—
a few scratched records—*Blind Faith, The Young Rascals,*

Blood on the Tracks—& seven paperbacks on the history
of philosophy written by a Jesuit priest. Carefully inscribed

inside each, in blue block letters, is my brother's name.
But tonight, because that set is on a shelf in another state,

the closest I can get to him is to listen again to a hissy recording
of a BBC debate, six decades old, between Copleston & Russell:

their argument over an argument—one of Aquinas's proofs
for the existence of God.

     Simply because we can name a thing,

Russell asserts—take the round square, for instance—
does not mean that it exists.

     This is what I think as I say *doyo*—

a word a friend has given me so that I might better understand
my own dizzy head this first week of September. For *doyo*

is not, as it is so often translated now, *the dog-days of summer*,
but rather *the fifth season,*

>   a season between seasons, those days,

after the rains have passed, when, centuries ago on the other side
of the world, everyone understood that it was necessary to carry

everything—scrolls & linens, shoes, even the wooden stools—
outside so they could be dried & cleansed

>   by the light.

Even the kimonos of the dead must be aired, Basho writes,
so that every yard was restrung with grief. And though there are

four fifth seasons, they, too, thought mostly of this one,
its afternoons of ripeness & loss, the harvest upon us,

or already past, the bushes becoming tinder—the chlorophyll
in the alders & maples giving way to the yellows & reds

of carotenoid & anthocyanin, so that soon, even as the engine
of the sun goes on roaring, the shoulders of the paths begin to fill

with bright leaves.

>   I have worn my mother's wedding ring

since before she died, since the day her fingers first swelled,

even as her arms & legs grew thinner.

>   Still, I am uncertain

whether or not, after so much time, it now feels as though it is

my own.

>   In a house I seal shut each autumn, there is a painting

by my father. When I return, the abstracted images of the horses

& riders, brushed directly onto plywood, are paler than I recall.

2.

Do you know the story of Little Bear? His mother bundling him

in a coat & hat to play in the snow, but these are not, in the end,
as warm as his own fur coat.

                         Soon I will take off even my skin.

And each loved thing will be lovingly held by someone
I have never met. This is, of course, the best-case scenario.

If this is the time of which Issa wrote *the wind chimes are silent,*
but the clocks still tick,
                       I would like to hold my contingent body

against the contingent body of the world, squeeze
the halved lemons with my thumbs, pare away the zest

with the smallest knife in the drawer.
                         Yesterday, without warning,
lightning took down a tree directly across the road

from where I was standing. The air was electric, but the sky
was blue.
              And last winter, one of my students, riding home

on his bike, was struck by a car driven by an 85-year-old man.
The driver leapt out & seeing him unhurt, grabbed the sides

of the boy's head, one palm to each ear, & pulled him toward him
& kissed his brow.
                  I would like to open again to the spot in the text

where my brother once underlined a proof for the existence
of angels—
            or the place he noted the dictum *not* on the primacy

of the intellect, but on the primacy of the will.
                         Today, I sank
into black dirt the roots of the chrysanthemums. I lifted the quilt

from the dryer & spread it on the bed.

Elsewhere neurologists
worked on the science of consciousness.

I find it easy

to both believe & not believe that *I think; therefore, I am.*

To imagine that this might be *the one & only day*—reality

intricately folded, everything always still infinitely possible,
even though we cannot yet grasp how.

Are we moving nearer or,

like the stars, farther apart?

Let us stand forehead to forehead,
for a long moment—*being* being as it is—as discrete & intimate

as the pages of a book. I want to turn again to the passage
in which it is explained how love is greater than knowledge.

Self-Portrait with No Shadow

My birth was a cloudless morning. Everything
was blue. My body was as round & gleaming
as a plate. Our island was as narrow & cold
as a blade. The first fruit I tasted was the donut
peach: its pit, a hard heart beneath a shroud
of meat. For a time, I lived between two brothers—
one with a door of iron; the other with no door
at all. For years their mouths were petals of silence
only I could understand. Their fingers, when they
put their hands in mine, were only so much
warm air. Our mother was a black Singer
sewing machine. Our father, a pair of red dice.
Our names, the dates of our births & deaths,
are snake eyes blown by the wind into the dunes
where rabbits burrow. My great-grandfather,
standing under a low sky in a distant land,
might have mistaken the waves for gray furrows,
as he petitioned the heavens for rain & sun
to turn the fields from ice to mud to green—
turnips & potatoes growing beneath the ground
like white & purple stones. As I child, I stole
my way into a maze of glass & mirrors. There
I bumped into myself at every turn; at every turn,
I tried to slip away. The minutes were a funhouse,
invisible walls against which I banged my nose.
The truth is my shadow will go on living forever
on that island no one can find, the island I am too
sad to visit. Each day it puts on all of the coats
I left behind, one atop the other, turns the collars up

& waits for the kettle to sing. It watches as a wren
tears a hole in the screen of the kitchen window
& carries off a thread of rusty wire in its beak.

FOUR

"There Will Never Be Another You"

Maybe everyone who ever wanted to be John Ashbery
can be John Ashbery now that John Ashbery is no longer
busy being himself. And maybe my former husband,
who was always on the lookout for a few good players
for a Steely Dan cover band, can be Walter Becker
now that Walter Becker is no longer available for gigs.
I tell myself I'm not interested in being anyone, though
I caught myself admitting over breakfast that the problem
with mortality is that l will genuinely miss myself
when I'm gone. If I were to pray, I would pray for the world
to find a way to put its seven & a half billon axes down.

Yesterday, a friend sent me a link to research that found
that under electroencephalographic study, the brains
of some people were no less moved by flowers
than they were by a human face, their brains lighting up
for objects as though the objects were alive. And so
I hold the hard pale body of my aging washing machine
in a tender embrace. We are dancing ourselves away
from the wall so that I can slip in behind it to install
a few feet of flexible hose. I am also putting in a valve
that will know to turn the water off, even if the machine—
wishing perhaps to be a water tower—asks for more
than it can hold. On the shelf John Ashbery's poems
go on being what they are. Just as beside them, in a book
about the Kunstkammer of Rudolf II, the emperor still
paces the ramparts of his castle, awaiting the four horsemen
who are bearing Dürer's "The Feast of the Rose Garlands"
from Venice to Prague. Classic rock radio stations will
go on playing "Peg," playing "Deacon Blues," though

Walter Becker can no longer spin vinyl to hear the tenor sax
of Dexter Gordon contrafacting "All the Things You Are,"
as I am doing now. The glass door of the wood stove
has never wanted to be a tangle of common milkweed,
though the afternoon sun brocades it with pink light.
In its iron belly, the day is already busy being spent.

America [April]

America, only yesterday it was the Easter ham
& bright asparagus with butter. It was the sweet
rice dish my favorite aunt used to feed us all.
It was the first long day of a new season of work,
hoisting quarters from our canvas change aprons
in a spring-cold arcade on a boardwalk in New Jersey
until it became the singular fullness I carry now,
the way my father seemed to carry his childhood
hunger, a tightness we could see between his ribs.
Once he told us how his father had walked in the dark
through a blizzard carrying a son in his arms.
How when he arrived at dawn at the doctor's door,
the fevered infant was already dead in its cradle
of wool. On Saturday, the neighborhood women
wrap whatever they can spare in blankets & carry it
to the park to set out on the grass to sell. One week
they call their plan *How to Pay for Electricity.*
The next, they say, *Let's Try to Fill the Car
with Gas.* Not because *Economic Sustainability*
is a less catchy name for a fast horse than *Joie
de Vivre,* but because there are limits to our means.
They blast Celine Dion from a boom box, duct tape
holding the batteries in place. And I would like
to talk to Czesław Miłosz about the words that
might save anything at all. At twenty-three, I was
already married. In another year my husband's
only sister would finally be killed by the tumor
she was carrying in her brain. She lay deaf & blind
& mute in a bed for months & because the light

of understanding must travel immeasurable distances,
it has taken her desolation decades to find me here
this morning, suddenly real & past imagining.
America, it must frighten you to study your great
shape in the black glass of the Atlantic. *Inoperable*
& *inevitable*, the surgeon explained. A small seed
she had borne since she was born. Before opening
his hands to make a sign like the great spiral nebula
of Andromeda, he lowered his index finger closer
& closer to his thumb to make the sign of the pea.

On the Eve of Spring Break

Daylight Savings. As though minutes might be bankable, as though there could be more or less of them simply by our agreeing to make it so. March weather: rain, then snow, then ice, then rain again, until our boots are as muddied as the terms a student, despairing in the chair beside my desk, recites from his tattered *Anthology of Theory & Criticism,* its one thousand onionskin leaves so thin the book seems more palimpsest than page. He says *post-human. Trans-species.* And I am suddenly thinking of Robinson Jeffers, thinking surely we would all be happier now just pushing a few boulders around. I am still halfway to another coast, imagining sea spray & sunlight, when the next student in the seat says she's just read we are all eight selves every time we speak. Then we consider whether the word before *other* in her opening stanza should be *each* or *an*—while I think now, for no apparent reason, of an old friend who waited a decade for her first husband to stop loving his second wife. If she had rediscovered within herself the young woman she once was, why hadn't he? Tomorrow, may we all be on a beach, sipping something sweet from a coconut, our flesh tuned for pleasure, the dazzled body churning out a warehouse of vitamin D. But, of course, most of us aren't that type. Soon we will repay our borrowed hours. But by then may even the ponderous be too drunk on the end of winter to care. It's simple: We'd rather set out in the dark than arrive there. If wisdom is a myth, it is one of the better ones. More exacting in its ways than love—for, unlike love, it schools us again & again in its own limitations.

Self-Portrait in Suspension

> This dewdrop world
> is a dewdrop world.
> And yet, and yet . . .
>
> —Kobayashi Issa

Because I have no one-quick-word for what I feel tonight
as a newscaster reports the beheading of an 82-year-old scholar
of antiquities in Palmyra—

              his mutilated body hung from a column

in the ancient square he loved—

                   I want back the hours I wasted
this afternoon seeking a pair of old-school Adidas Superstars.
The most mindful moments of my day passed as I waited

for a discount haircut. And later,
                I breathed deeply & slowly
as I watched brown bread brown in the toaster.
                     Yesterday,
a semi-automated phone call informed me of the compromise

of my identity, assured me my bank had preemptively blocked
all access to my funds. Panicked over how little cash I had,
I lost it,
        shuffling my cell phone in & out of my pocket

to make a dozen frantic & fruitless calls.
                 Now, after a dinner
of noodles & beans, I scoop Chinese herbs into warm water & drink,
knowing I could not pronounce the ingredients even if

I knew them, knowing some part of me knows it is foolish
to dose myself on trust alone,

                              knowing my former husband's cousin
would say this is how people end up with other people's kidneys.

A friend who consults the *I Ching* before each meal reminds me
to trust my intuition.
                         At fourteen, I named the mollies
in the small tank beside my bed Doc, Doc, & Doc because,

despite great effort, I could never learn to tell them apart.
One morning, while I was at school studying biology or algebra,
the charcoal filter backed up & they died.
                                   How common

the belief that each of us matters. How unfathomable the fact
that our urgent *being* ends.
                    I have no one-quick-word
for my feelings for the hip kids in the park who call all their dogs

Dog.
     And so, when the crows gather in the yard to pick
at the scattered tops of strawberries & apple cores, I open a book
at random to name them.
                       Sometimes I lift the old blue paperback

of *Common Wild Flowers* & read from it a litany of the words
for the world we have been given by those who came before:
Keck & *Traveller's Joy. Violet. Primrose. Nightshade, Nettle,*

Shepherd's-purse. Honeysuckle, Broom.
                           If to name is an act
of owning, perhaps to list is to spend or to sow. Profligate.

The beauty of the light at dusk sluices the mind with sorrow—

or so the latest research suggests.
                     Here, in the growing darkness,
the white trees are blooming, the forsythia, the daffodils.
                                 The dryer
buzzes—like a bell, & not—just once, at the far corner of the house.

59

The small motor of the refrigerator kicks on. Elsewhere,
a 2,000-year-old temple is being blasted into dust.

And yet. . . .

I open *The Complete Book of Patience Games*, say *Pendulum.*

Little Spider. Napoleon at St. Helena. Crescent. Captive. Clock.

Twilight. And that's the thing, isn't it? A phrase, coming back:
To say two things at once.

Outside, the sky is saying its two things—

more, no more, more, no more—

Fierce lullaby. A last careful crow
paces, bowing its head as it goes; every step, a seeming genuflection.

Passage

Praise you for saying you will never know
a single thing anyone ever thinks or feels.
I, too, think & feel this way. When
my mother's father died of tuberculosis,
her mother went to work in a hospital kitchen,
feeding her four children for years
on the sick's uneaten meals. Today, mine
is the last car in line to board the ferry.
Only once was I the first to be left behind.
Ten minutes out of the harbor & we are all
already rocking & green. And if, beyond this
small nausea, somewhere within me,
my body is already plotting its own end,
that's another interiority I don't know
a thing about. When I finally tracked down
the woman who had abandoned my father
& his brother, she was ninety, living
in a trailer park outside Miami Beach.
I asked but she could not remember
her mother's maiden name. She'd closed
the door behind her one night forever—
she wanted me to understand the story
fully—because her husband had called her
Monkey Face. Monkey Face, your children
gone then into the orphanages, then
the cold fields of a farm north of Albany,
gone into the machines of Domino Sugar.
Oh, Monkey Face. My father's father's name
also lost, cast out of the Lithuanian

he refused to speak in America—even though
this rendered him mute & inscrutable—
into something only a non-Pole would think
was Polish. Praise that it does not hurt
more than it does, that it is bearable, to be
a rusted link in a busted chain. They came
separately at fourteen. Alone on different
boats. It was the twentieth century.
Their villages, two docks, waving them off
into an idea more alien than eternity.

When my mother's grandmother eloped
with an English soldier, her Irish family
gave the couple one-way tickets
to the New World & money enough
to buy a cow in Delaware. I've never known
any more than this. All of it half-true at best.
Less than the echo of a squeak in the din.
Sometimes a pod of dolphins, like a rash
of the miraculous, breaks the surface of the bay.
But not this morning. The captain announces
high winds, rough water. Still, I feel exactly
one person less lonely. Starboard, brother,
precisely, I see a different sea than you see.

    —For Matthew Zapruder

A Short History of Sorrow

It isn't true that the evening crashes down. Certainly
not tonight, as it drops instead to the fern-covered rim
of the lake like tufts of down—the horizon's molt, rouge
at first, then jaundiced, then blue, then gray. We have
folded another day's complicated news & wonder
whether it might not yet be possible for pure ineptitude
to save us all—both from those sorrows that seem
almost unremarkable & all the others that do not.
This morning, we passed a fallen nest, its mossy belly
still cradling a speckled clutch of unbroken eggs.
A few days before, a fist-sized turtle, trailing blood,
dragged itself across the road. Yet when I spoke
to my friend at noon, she seemed calm as she described
from her suburban window a frantic fawn lurching
from lawn to lawn unable to find its mother. Perhaps
we relearn daily to endure what we cannot change.
The man I love tells me researchers do not use the word
intelligence for the feats some birds can do because
intelligence seems too human. *Cognition,* he says,
is what they like to say about the raven's abilities—
to pick a lock with a tool, to remember the tool, to plan,
to choose the right tool again later, to choose the key
to future food over a morsel of food offered now.
And so it is a joke when I go on calling the small lizard—
who repeatedly throws itself into the pool from which
I repeatedly fish it out—in turns, *dumb & suicidal.*

When I ask, the man I love explains the chemistry
of *surfactants.* When I ask how one actually performs
chest compressions on a newborn, he holds up

the second & third fingers of his right hand. We are
together now because both of our former spouses decided
after thirty years that they were through. Tonight,
he is telling me the story of a man who lives on a ranch
in Mexico with fifty stray dogs he's taken in, a man
who has not seen his only son since the boy was two.
Years ago, he killed a woman in a car accident
& almost died himself. He'd been drinking. He'd gone
from last call to his car to a coma, to a court, to a cell,
then back to a silent house on the dusty land
from which he'd come. Sometimes there is no way
to make a sad story assert anything beyond its grief.

Here, away from the sea, even as the sun goes down,
the air feels hot & heavy. This morning three doves
flew hard into the glass, their necks snapping on impact,
their feathers—soft silver, pink, white—blasted
to the far end of the deck. Now a few tiny finches bully
one another at the feeders filled with the thistle seeds
they love. When a small Cessna or Piper passes over
on its way to the county airport, we do not expect
missiles or canisters of sarin gas. Perhaps we are writing
a short history of happiness, for we each seem amazed
simply to be able to reach out & touch the other's cheek.
Who can doubt that suffering arises from our attachment
to what cannot last? The sparrow's high song is such
clean music. The tops of the trees sway in the wind—
like shadow puppets—against the sky's hushed ticking.

FIVE

Here, After

When she was walking this morning, a pair of martins
darted from a tree & swept past her ears, one on each side,
so that she thought maybe the marriage had been like that,
two sets of wings, the color of twilight, on either side
of an idea no more substantial than the picture of the sky
the lake gives back—mesmerizing, changing, abiding,
but also unreal, even though the lake has somehow held
the sky within it for as long as it can remember
in the only way it knows how. She remembers the parrot
a childhood friend had owned, how it would call
the girl's mother in the voice of her father & her father
in the voice of her mother, the one or the other shouting
What? What? before finally bursting into the room
where only the bird stood, cocking its head as it talked
to itself in its cage. Maybe it had been like that—
but without the bird. Yes, she thinks, no bird,
though possibly the cage. Or, if the lake thinks, *Shoreline
is just another word for embrace*, maybe the sky can't
understand why the lake seems to never show its true face,
why, though each drop of water is transparent, it seems
to always be hiding its depths. Even the mist they conjure
sometimes between them is not the fine suspension
either of them believes mist might be. One day the parrot
learned to imitate perfectly the sound of the telephone
ringing so that soon everyone was rushing to lift the receiver,
heavy as a hope, saying *Hello? Hello?*—thrilled, then
disappointed. Was there another world outside calling
more, more, more? Now, in bed alone, the house so quiet,
she thinks of that book that concludes with a man singing,

67

low, without accompaniment, in his kitchen: *This train
ain't a going-home train, this train.* And she thinks the marriage
had been like that, whistling its own refrain: *already gone.*

Death Dream in August

See! I give myself to you, Beloved!

—Amy Lowell

Sometimes we cannot shake off so swiftly the visions of the night before: a doctor surgically removing my mouth, giving me two weeks to live—*these will be the days*, she says, *without food or words*. On the operating table, counting down, I tell myself that when I come to I will be over the shock & terror. I will merely be unfathomably sad. The office is a yellow carnival. Someone is taking a picture. The dog is wearing a set of Mickey Mouse ears. When they look at this picture, years from now, I think, someone will say, *Oh, that was the day they took out her mouth*, but I won't be there. By noon, I can recite all the reasons I may have dreamt what I did: a friend who is gravely ill, a father-in-law who has become a stranger to himself. A too-spicy dinner. The existential facts. Kafka. But not the body trying to tell me something. Not the universe. Not a message from a god. They say that when they removed the spiked shackle & heavy links from the foot of an elephant chained to a tree in India for fifty years, the animal wept. When, in the wild, they finger with their trunks the clean bones in their graveyards, what do they think? Parked at the drive-through window, waiting for a kale salad with goat cheese & nuts, I check my phone. And there is Amy Lowell again, giving me—the-poem-of-the-day—once more the generous gift of herself. A triple-digit sun glares on the empty turnpike. Dry leaves already litter the grass. Chickadees in the morning. At dusk, deer too young to be afraid. A friend promises to text the design of her new tattoo, a calla lily on her wrist. *Memento mori*, she writes. I punch out letters imperfectly with one finger. Language, Heidegger thought, is thought's experience of itself. I woke at dawn hugging my body, as though it might be possible to keep myself warm.

Self-Portrait with Moon

The solstice is behind us, but the days are still short
& dark, the sun erasing itself hours before dinner
hits the table. I am thinking about something
in a cast iron pan. Isn't that how things work?
The year my marriage ended I went to bed as early
as I could in order to maximize my experience
of daylight. In other words, I was trying not to reach
down into some pit for that round empty weight,
that enormous ergonomic handle. For it was inside
just such a skillet, I think, that my mother stirred
her dissatisfaction. And now that I am middle-aged,
I have no idea why my parents didn't get along.
Why each of us seems to wake some mornings
asking, *Why can't I just do whatever I want?*

Somewhere in Antarctica a man is setting out alone
on foot. He has left behind his wife & children.
These adventures, he says, *are very selfish odysseys.*
He has a sled but no dogs. He wants to pull the sled
himself. He plans to cross a continent hauling
everything he will need for the journey behind him
in orange sacks. For years I had hair to my waist
& what I wanted was for a man to want to brush it
every night for the rest of our lives. I thought that
that was how love must feel. Soft boar bristles
pulling the oil through until each strand shone.

It is too easy to chalk up this evening's restlessness—
the view of the birdfeeders already gone black—
to the ghost of someone else's old unhappiness:

Think *epigenetic discontent.* But isn't this just
one of those moments in which, for no reason,
nothing feels right? Only a few hours earlier,
the sky was the wing of an eastern bluebird.
I looked up into it & said aloud, *Try to remember
this.* I have a friend who cannot understand how love
comes to an end. When she asks, I have no reply.
When I hold her question under the lamp later,
I see only my own hands. Last night, the moon was
so bright, so close, that the grass, dusted with white
light, threw down a thousand crisp, thin shadows,
& I stood on my front step as though it were a stage.

America [emptiness]

The presence of a middle ear is not a necessary condition
for terrestrial hearing.

—Renaud Boistel et al.

America, my older brother had huge feet.
Perhaps this is what you need to hear. Or
that he sometimes shook one or the other
savagely when he sat, his legs crossed
at the ankles or the knees, though I don't
know why. Both of my feet could easily fit
into one of his shoes. And did. For a long time,
I have carried a great coldness that once
belonged to him. When he died, it somehow
slid in. I had my head on his chest because
it was hard to tell if his heart was still
beating. His breaths had gotten so far apart.
Like a hunter with an ear to the brown earth,
or a child, maybe imitating something
he'd seen a cartoon character do, putting
a small ear to the iron track. Home
from college for the first time, he sat
in my bedroom & told me the story
of the scholar who, relentlessly seeking
wisdom, visits a monk. When the monk
fills the man's cup with tea, he fills it
to overflowing. The scholar becomes alarmed,
but the monk continues to pour. Today,
after four unsuccessful attempts,
a sixty-four-year-old woman will swim
from Cuba to the Florida Keys. My brother

was dead at 43. For a time, he wanted
to be a priest. And, once, our mother was
very cruel to him. She refused to accept
a gift he had made for her at school.
I cannot explain it: I was so small myself—
a decade younger—peering down
into our silvery living room, watching him
cry. On an island in the Indian Ocean,
there is a frog so tiny, it has no room
in its skull for a tympanic middle ear.
Scientists, assuming it was deaf,
were stunned to discover that
when played recordings of other frogs
croaking, the Gardiner frog croaked back.
And so it has only just now become
known to us: this creature who listens
to the world through its opened mouth.
America, I am telling you this because
I would like to feel warm. Enough is
enough. Perhaps the cure is not to say
everything but rather to say each day
one small thing we have only just now
discovered we had forgotten we knew.

Greetings from Richmond (or Thinking of Elizabeth Bishop & Everything Else in the World)

I walk from one room in the house to another & the dog follows.

Sometimes
when I sit, he sits beside me, puts his wide paw on my knee—his devotion,

a heavy gift.

This afternoon, in the acupuncturist's apothecary, I scanned—
as he mixed the herbs—the shelves of labeled bottles. *Magic Three*

& *Happy Liver. The Noble Ones. I want JOY*, I joke & am told I will get it,
though there was a time last spring when it would have been more

than I could stand. For when he pressed his hand to my sternum
& said *heart,*

I felt not only the ache of the pericardium but also the ache

of something else.

Shen, some ancient text might say. At home in the kitchen,
I stir the powder into a cup of warm water & look out to the dark line

along the creek, the twenty towering cypress trees the arborist has said
are dying.

And though this is only rented land, the gloom feels overwhelming.

The holly, too, seems to be browning. The rock rose, a boxwood, the azaleas.
Asked *why*, the expert simply shrugged, the way someone would

who did not need to be reminded that even the evergreen is mortal.

Tonight,
the moon is nearly full, the sky clear, the temperature sweetly falling,

by which, in fact, I still mean *joy,*

though this is one of the lesser species—

hybrid, chimera,

     appreciation, even awe, grafted onto grief. The black tongues

of the trees still hum with the cicada's call, are still haunted now & then
by the tremulous *hoo* of the owl.

       I whisper into the ears of their long shadows:

How tired I am of death & how tired I am of flailing against it.

         Last week,

when I saw a tiny spider clinging to its frail web near the door of the shower,

I stepped out, wet & naked, in order to carry it outside,

        while somewhere

in Austria, police were opening the rear doors of a truck to find the bodies

of the seventy-one refugees who had suffocated inside.

      Sometimes,

in search of some insight, I read again the words of one master or another

so that in this way I have learned I might yet become a formless field
of benefaction, learned, too, that my desire will likely have no end.

Hence, when the same old orange pickup—model year 1970? 1975?—
passes by as I walk the dog at sunset, I still think

      if there were a vehicle

in which one might escape into enlightenment, surely that would be the one.
Bishop, studying the silver sea beside the fishhouses, imagines

that knowledge, if we could touch it, would be so cold it would seem
at first to burn, *a transmutation of fire.*

     When I look for a long minute

into the face of my dog, I know there is another world—
immediate, un-languaged—into which I cannot travel.

       If I could save

the trees—perhaps by climbing high up inside the branches
to wash each weeping canker with a rag dipped in some milky salve—

I like to think that I would try. But the arborist says again & again, *essentially untreatable*, by which he means *doomed*.

And because

the trees are, he guesses, thirty years old, even if young ones
were planted here tomorrow, I would not live long enough to see them

grow this tall.

When we say *wisdom*, perhaps this is what we mean.

Postscript from the Heterochronic-Archipelagic Now

The sun is new each day.

—Heraclitus

After seasons of neglect, I am giving the gardenia my most faithful
observance—an acidic fertilizer, ample water, & this consistent bath

of moderate sun, in which I am now considering the perforations
a colony of aphids exacted last winter on a pair of waxy leaves,

admiring the elegant execution of their need. This was before
I knew to spray the whole thing down with soap & water.

Before I knew it likes the damp so much it will only thrive
when misted daily. No wonder it has been years since it has put forth

a bud.
            In another life, I once held a palm-sized chip of driftwood
shipworms had laced in just this way. I can still peer through it

in my mind, but I cannot raise it up, here, today, in this quiet light.
Yet, sometimes it seems as though I have only just now set it down,

beside the thin gold bangle my mother gave me, on a little table,
beside the iron bed in which I used to sleep.
                                        Yesterday a student said,

I do not know what you mean when you say image. My stories,
she insisted, *are only made of words.* Sometimes, I can almost imagine

America as an idea I can address directly, as in *America, you, too,*
must sometimes feel like an imperfectly grafted hothouse flower.

Or I can almost imagine myself this way, the self I once was, as remote
& lonely as the idea of a country no letter can reach.

                                        So that when

I say *you,* or even *she* or *her,* I often mean *me,* or *I,* as in that other self,
that *you* I used to be.

                    As in *you* who cannot know—huddled as you are

there, in the dark, your husband en route to a psych ward, the electricity,
the gas, even the cellular service shut off for failure to pay—

that all of this will pass.

                        For wasn't it just last week I passed
the wife of a colleague weeping in the hall outside his office door?

Wasn't it only a month ago someone first suggested he seemed
confused? Heartbreaking was the one word she could compose

herself to utter, as she slipped by with a box of photos & books.

                                                    And

I think of a friend's astonishing copies of Fitzgerald & Hemingway,

the simple yellowing paperbacks he's carried for decades, bound now
with rubber bands—the margins overflowing, dog-ears marking

every turn of the plot.

                    In another century Faulkner wrote, *The past
is never dead.* Yet new news arrives each morning in its plastic sleeve

at the end of the long drive, & I open to troops amassing on a border,
open to a child behind chain link grasping—not a mother's hem

but the silver corner of a Mylar rescue sheet.

                                        The *words-of-the-years*
slide along: from *refudiate* to *post-truth. Selfie. Emoji.* Maybe once

simulacrum. Once the pronoun *they,* now the metaphor—*dumpster fire,*
if not *shithole.*

            At any moment, we might hear someone proclaim,

The truth is not the truth.

Though it must be. Though we have to live as though it is.

We recall the *known-knowns.* The *Unknown-unknowns.*

Until . . . you know.

Yet, I am here, which means *you* are here. Look, how gently, how carefully, we are misting the gardenia.

If such attention

can, as the latest studies show, change the amygdala, it still goes on failing to change the world.

Later, I will toss out scraps—the tops

of carrots & radishes, a few fists of wilted greens—for the rabbits & deer. Sometimes, in the late afternoon, I can spot them beyond

the fence, but I cannot hold them. Cannot gather up the indigo bunting. The yellow finch. Or Spring, its skin of dew on the grass.

Somewhere there is a *you* so cold she cannot stop shaking. *She* checks the thermostat with a flashlight, though there is, of course, nothing

she can do. *You* would turn on the heat, if there were heat. Or light the stove. *You* would put on a hat & walk to your parents' house,

if they weren't already dead. Look, *she* is putting the letter, unopened, & the life insurance policy back in a drawer.

She has yet to turn

out the pockets of every coat, yet to search the bottom of every purse for money to buy a cheap burner phone & a few hours of talk.

A *you* who is only just now waking up to that life in which our shadow will forever go on living. Or maybe *she* is the shadow.

Or *I* am.

After all, I have sometimes mistaken an old nest for a bird. Though earlier, I thought the flutter of a waxwing was a dry leaf

still holding on somehow to a branch. When I step out into the garage, I realize I have left the hanging florescent light on again all night.

79

Energy. Spent. Gone.

Sometimes the old dog licks one paw until
it bleeds. *Common,* the vet says, but not easy to explain.

The editorial

atop the recycling bin asks, *What does this moment demand?*
On the hill, the black haw is blooming—each cyme, each opening,

a cluster of selves. And, here, the river birch is peeling. Somewhere a *you*
cannot even imagine this. *Imagine.* We have never seen a thing

like this before. Its shedding bark, like ruined pages, curls & falls away.

A Rhetoric

It is hard to contend with passion; for whatever it desires,
it buys at the cost of the soul.

—Heraclitus

They that are awake have one world in common,
but of the sleeping each turns aside into a world
of his own.

—Heraclitus

Or how *how we say what we say* says everything
we don't actually say but somehow mean, even if
what we mean is, frankly, very mean & not in the end
what we thought we intended. Not simply chiasmus
or pathos or logos but more than anyone can imagine:
visual rhetoric, virtual rhetoric, vernacular rhetoric,
cultural rhetoric, the rhetoric of the first-person shooter,
the rhetoric of the team, the mediated landscape, disputed
landscape, the rhetoric of the drone. The rhetoric
of soundscapes, soundtracks, sound effects: each click
of a keyboard, the clatter of the skateboard, the chatter
of the switchboard, & the rhetoric of the closed captioning
whose scrolling announces *Today the government is closed,*
that says, *Let us welcome the new Minister of Loneliness.*

Imagine a field composed of the crosshatches
of hashtags, like crop circles in prairies waiting
to be mined by an algorithm for big data, a domain
asking to be drilled down into so that we can understand
what we already assume we understand. The rhetoric
of media: new, social, mass, & multimodal. Snapchat,
Instagram. Twitter. Friend me. The rhetoric of the post-
truth, post-human bot. Somewhere an engineer
of ether is upgrading the remoteness of the academy,
the incredulity of the fourth estate while I listen
to my dog chew an antler. The moon is a thin rung
in an empty tree. The snow, glowing at night, could be
a radiant, unread scripture from another world.

Weeks ago our neighbor killed himself. When I walk
past his house tonight, the motion detectors illuminate
the deck & the drive. His porch light, which he set
with a timer, dutifully continues to turn itself on. There
is his pickup & his station wagon. Inside the garage,
the vintage yellow Mustang upon whose gas pedal
he piled a stack of bricks. Surely, there is a rhetoric
for suicide. This I know, even if what I know is only
what I have gleaned from a letter I never opened.
The rhetoric of the lacuna, the refusal, the not-wanting-
to-know. When I walk past, I hear the soft peep
of a downed bird, but I cannot find it, the call carrying
so cleanly through the cold it is hard to tell the direction
from which it comes. We all care about survival.
We all know helplessness & grief. Recognize grace.
A rhetoric of persistence, assistance, charity, catastrophe,
epidemic. The rhetoric that inoculates or will not be
inoculated. A rhetoric that resists change & a rhetoric
that resists the resistance. Rhetoric, colonizing,
decolonizing, universal, unique, moving toward category
collapse, toward a reconstruction of gender & race,
ability, disability, that is ever more *inter, hybrid, trans.*

Still, across the lake, someone is shooting a shotgun
into the starlight or into a bale of hay. The teenager
delivering a pizza cocks his head, winks, says, *Now
that's some real country music.* The rhetoric of territory,
of *This Land Is My Land*, of *No Trespassing*, of *Danger:
Hunting.* I could be at any moment—like the woman
killed with one clean shot while walking her retriever—
mistaken for something wilder than I am, even as
I look down, distracted by the blown kiss emoticon
you are sending me from your seat on the plane
as one flight attendant shuts the door & another
prepares to review the safety features of your Airbus,
your Embraer, your 777. When you drive up later,
how happy you will be to see our other neighbor
has replaced the Confederate flag hanging in his yard
with one with snowflakes & a cardinal, even as
a student in the back row of her theory class says, *Wait.*

Isn't that a sign? Everyone on board has passed
through security, has been patted down by the rhetoric
of terror, of scrutiny, of surveillance, of suspicion.
The rhetoric of color, I mean literal color, the widest
implications of red, white, & blue. The rhetoric of orange,
of high alert. The rhetoric of scent, of bomb sniffing,
of plants, an eco-rhetoric, the rhetoric of the molecular
fingerprint. The rhetoric of brown. And because my mind
is so heavy with how we cannot help bludgeoning
each other with the shapes of our ideas, I need to imagine
a scholar two rows up, who will, when the flight reaches
its cruising altitude, turn on the tiny overhead lamp
& drop his tray table to begin again to devotedly translate
love letters that have never been translated before—
the language the writers used so old, so opaque, so alien,
it feels almost new—meaning un-coded, unloaded, benign.

But this isn't about us. This is about the love of the tongue
for the word & for the other & the *other* other. The rhetoric
of ethos, ethics, the rhetoric of soul. And so the scholar
is thinking now of persuasion, not as an instrument
of violence & muscle but as one of mystery, diplomacy,
delight. Someone says what she cannot understand is how
the neighbor left his dog behind. The retired homicide detective
who lives five houses down found it wandering. He said
he knew almost at once, from the behavior, the bark, the owner
was dead. Rhetoric of frenzy, friendship. Of the creature,
of fur. A rhetoric civic & civil. Our most elemental fears
& needs. Sometimes it is hard to tell a plea from a command.
The rhetoric of treats, treaties, entreaties. When he said quietly
sit, the dog sat. The rhetoric of rescue, of longing & belonging,
the lover, the beloved. A rhetoric of oneness or none-ness.
A rhetoric of everyone simply wanting everyone to stay.

Acknowledgments

I am deeply grateful for the generous support I have received from the John Simon Guggenheim Foundation, the National Endowment for the Arts, and the American Academy of Arts and Letters. I am also grateful to Virginia Commonwealth University and to my students and my colleagues in the Department of English, especially my fellow poets David Wojahn and Greg Donovan. I am also very lucky to have had more distant families during the long years it has taken me to complete this manuscript: my love and gratitude to my colleagues at the Vermont College of Fine Arts Post-Graduate Writing Conference and those in the low-residency MA in Creative Writing and Literature for Educators Program at Fairleigh Dickinson University.

I am thankful to the following journals for offering such good homes to the following poems: "The Fifth Season," "Impasto for the Parietal," "Death Dream in August," "Self-Portrait with No Shadow," and "Labyrinth," *Parhelion Literary Magazine*; "Greetings from Wildwood," *Cortland Review*; "Self-Portrait in Suspension" and "The Year of the Horse," *Washington Square*; "Self-Portrait with Moon" and "A Rhetoric," *Solstice*; " 'There Will Never Be Another You,' " "Here, After," and "America: Flight," *Plume*; "New Year" and "Beginner's Mind," *AGNI*; " 'The Weight,' " *The Literary Review*; "America [superstorm]," *The New Republic*; "America [peaches]," "The Zeitgeist Bird," "Passage," and "America [April]," *American Poetry Review*; "The River Twice," *Painted Bride Quarterly*; "America [train]," *Gulf Coast*; "Bitter Vetch" and "Self-Portrait with No Internal Navigation," *Mead*.

I owe an incalculable debt to Renee Ashley, for without her assistance and absolute insistence this manuscript would never have been completed. And many thanks to Laura McCullough and Anthony Carelli, who have read and commented on so many versions of so many of these poems, and to Matt Donovan, who also generously read the whole darn thing. The love and encouragement of my brother and his family—Francis Kaklauskas and Elizabeth Olson and their son Levi—sustain me.

Notes

I first encountered the fragments of the pre-Socratic philosopher Heraclitus of Ephesus (c. 535–c. 475 BCE) as an undergraduate majoring in philosophy at Hofstra University. Even in his own time, Heraclitus's ideas were considered obscure and his character was described as melancholy. No original text of his work has survived, and what is known comes to us through brief passages quoted (or closely paraphrased) in the works of others. These scattered fragments, once compiled, point in several directions. They advance, on the one hand, his belief in a singular pervasive force that orders all things (logos), while asserting, on the other hand, that all things are in a constant state of change. One might conclude from this that such flux (the river's continual flowing, for instance, or the continual psychic change within a person stepping into it) is not contrary to the nature of the cosmos but rather fundamental to it, and Heraclitus was, in this way, surely one of the first thinkers to recognize the ontological concept of *becoming*, as opposed to the fixed idea of *being*. The governing design of the universe seems to be, according to his philosophy, embodied in the tensions between opposites and in mutations across a small set of elemental states of being. All of this, in turn, he believed, produces (or is at least capable of producing) a kind of harmony. How all of this might or might not be supported by current ideas of physics or metaphysics, neurology or psychology, is for others to speculate. For my part, I can only say that these enigmatic fragments remain haunting, provocative, and poetic. The text that I read decades ago was Philip Wheelwright's translations and commentary, *Heraclitus* (Princeton University Press, 1959), and I have used those translations here. I have in one case (the opening epigraph) positioned two very closely related fragments together. In one case (*Oxen are happy when they find bitter vetches to eat*, sometimes identified as Fragment 4), I relied upon John Burnet's equally seminal translations, as I could not readily locate this fragment among those translated by Wheelwright.

"Self-Portrait with No Internal Navigation" refers to the Cape May–Lewes Ferry, which crosses the Delaware Bay between southern New Jersey and southern Delaware, roughly between Cape May Point and Cape Henlopen. Philippe Petit walked between the Twin Towers of the World Trade Center in

New York City on August 7, 1974. Information about this event comes primarily from the 2008 documentary *Man on Wire*.

"The Weight" is dedicated to Alistair Jones. It takes its name from the song of the same name by The Band. The epigraph is a quote from The Band's guitarist Robbie Robertson as reported by Rob Bowman. This passage in which Robertson discusses the various inspirations for the song has been quite widely distributed, but it seems to have first appeared in the article "Life Is a Carnival" in *Goldmine Magazine*, July 26, 1991. The Norwegian novel mentioned here is, of course, *My Struggle* by Karl Ove Knausgård. The Byrd Theater is in Richmond, Virginia. "Swinging on a Star" was composed by Jimmy Van Heusen and Johnny Burke. It was introduced by Bing Crosby in the 1944 film *Going My Way.*

"Self-Portrait with *The Sleeping Man*" references a photograph by Markéta Luskačová (https://www.lgp.cz/en/event/exhibition/photographs-19642014 .html#prettyPhoto[detail]/2/). The photo, taken in 1968, is also referred to as *Sleeping Pilgrim.*

On January 27, 2018, a Taliban suicide bomber killed more than 100 people and wounded at least 235 in Kabul, the Afghan capital. The bomber had disguised his vehicle to look like an ambulance.

"America [flight]" contains an epigraph that appeared, as indicated, in the *New York Times.* The publication date was January 19, 2013.

"New Year" contains an epigraph that appeared online at Space.com on February 5, 2015.

"Beginner's Mind" takes its title from the classic text *Zen Mind, Beginner's Mind* by Shunryu Suzuki and contains italicized fragments from that text. This poem also references *My So-Called Life*, a television series that aired for one season only, from August 25, 1994 to January 26, 1995. The show starred Claire Danes and Jared Leto as high school students. There is also a teeny-weeny snippet of Neil Young's song "Hey Hey, My My (Into the Black)." Bill Murray and Scarlett Johansson starred in the 2003 film *Lost in Translation.* Murray's final lines to Johansson are intentionally inaudible (indecipherable) to viewers.

"America [train]" references the Equity Strategy memo issued at Citigroup on October 16, 2005. Written by three analysts (Ajay Kapur, Niall Macleod, Narendra Singh), the memo's abstract opens with the following sentence: "The World is dividing into two blocs—the Plutonomy and the rest." By their definition, a plutonomy is an economy "where economic growth is powered by and largely consumed by the wealthy few." Greystone is Greystone Park Psychiatric Hospital located in Morristown, New Jersey. Seventeen year-old Anna Beninati's legs were severed at the knees on September 5, 2011 while she was trying to hop a freight train in Longmont, Colorado.

"Bitter Vetch" contains a pretty obvious reference to Mary Shelley's novel *Frankenstein.*

"The Zeitgeist Bird" is dedicated to Anthony Carelli, who sent me the epigraph as a writing prompt. It is from *Imperium* by Ryszard Kapuściński, the Polish journalist (born in Belarus, 1932–2007) whose absolute reliability has frequently been questioned. He himself said of his project that he was more interested in the essence of a matter than in merely making certain that all the details add up. The Battle of Hastings was fought on October 14, 1066 between the Norman-French army of William, the duke of Normandy, and the English army of Anglo-Saxon king Harold Godwinson. It marks the beginning of the Norman conquest of England. The DMV refers to the Department of Motor Vehicles. The Bayeux Tapestry is approximately 230 feet long. It is displayed in Bayeux, France, and is believed to date from the eleventh century. It depicts the Battle of Hastings.

"Labyrinth" contains an earworm from the Michael Bublé song "Home." What can I say? Popular music finds its way into us all.

"America [October]" refers to CERN, the European Organization for Nuclear Research. CERN operates the largest particle physics laboratory in the world. The Hadron Collider is a part of its accelerator complex.

"Impasto for the Parietal" has an epigraph from *The Mind in the Cave: Consciousness and the Origins of Art*, a 2002 study of Upper Paleolithic European rock art written by the archaeologist David Lewis-Williams. The passage is a quote from an interview with the students (local cavers, including Jean-Marie Chauvet, for whom the Chauvet Cave is now named) who discovered the cave paintings in Ardèche, France. This discovery was made in December 1994. The italicized words in the opening lines of section 1 are also taken from that interview as reported by Lewis-Williams. Section 2 references the essay "The Places Below" by Loren Eiseley, the American anthropologist and natural scientist. The italicized fragments are from his book *The Night Country.*

Ferdinand de Saussure was a Swiss linguist. Sigmund Freud was an Austrian neurologist and the founder of psychoanalysis. The Cave of Altamira is renowned for its numerous parietal cave paintings. The earliest paintings in the cave were executed approximately 36,000 years ago.

"The River Twice" contains an italicized paraphrase of a government letter regarding a mandatory adjustment to the formula used to calculate unemployment compensation. The regulations governing unemployment extensions during a recession are apparently quite complex (you can get an idea of this from a 2013 Congressional Research Service document, "Extending Unemployment Compensation Benefits during Recessions," https://fas.org/sgp/crs/misc/RL34340.pdf).

The fragment from Heraclitus pertaining to the bow and the lyre is this one: *Men do not know how what is at variance agrees with itself. It is an attunement of opposite tension, like that of the bow and the lyre.* I regret that have no idea from which gospel songs these lines might come.

"America [superstorm]" references Hurricane (or Superstorm) Sandy, the most catastrophic storm of the 2012 Atlantic hurricane season. It affected 24 states, causing nearly $70 billion in damage. The most severe damage occurred along the coasts of New Jersey and New York. This poem also discusses game theory, which is commonly defined as the study of mathematical models of conflict and cooperation between intelligent rational decision-makers. Unfortunately, I do not remember which specific essay on game theory I read before I wrote this poem. On December 14, 2012, Adam Lanza opened fire at the Sandy Hook Elementary School in Newtown, Connecticut. He killed 20 children between the ages of six and seven. After learning that they would soon go blind, deaf twin brothers from Belgium chose to be euthanized (at the age of 45) because they couldn't bear the thought of not being able see one another. Marc and Eddy Verbessem of Putte died December 14, 2013 by lethal injection at Brussels University Hospital. My brother passed away on October 21, 1995 from lung cancer. He was 43.

"Landscape with No One in It" references the popular song "Autumn Leaves." It was originally composed with French lyrics in 1945 (music by Hungarian-French composer Joseph Kosma and lyrics by Jacques Prévert). It is now an American standard that has been recorded many times by a wide variety of artists. Monastral blue is the commercial name for a synthetic pigment derived from phthalocyanine.

"Greetings from Wildwood" ends with a gesture toward (and a few italicized words from) James Wright's famous poem "A Blessing." Daredevil is a Marvel superhero. Swamp Thing, on the other hand, appears in DC Comics. The italics indicate lines from a poem written by my younger brother (Francis Kaklauskas). The ethicist here is the British philosopher Derek Parfit. The quote is from his 2011 work *On What Matters.*

"America [Assateague]" begins with a line from Walker Percy's classic essay "The Loss of the Creature." The italicized words near the end of the poem are from John Berger's essay "Why Look at Animals."

"The Fifth Season" has a long and convoluted epigraph (In fact, the convolution of this passage is for me the greatest part of its pleasure) from the second volume of Frederick Copleston's *A History of Philosophy* (1946). The BBC debate between Bertrand Russell and Copleston regarding Thomas Aquinas's proofs for the existence of God is available on YouTube (https://www.youtube .com/watch?v=hXPdpEJk78E).

Dr. Elson Haas gives a fairly clear explanation of *doyo* in "Late Summer and the Doyo" (https://omtimes.com/2018/09/late-summer-doyo/).

Little Bear is a children's classic published in 1957. Oh, how I loved this book! It was written by Else Holmelund Minarik and illustrated by Maurice Sendak. "I think; therefore, I am" is, of course, the famous Cartesian assertion. The haiku of Basho and Issa are of course very widely available. "The one and only day" is not meant to quote from or refer to any particular text.

"There Will Never Be Another You" is a popular song written in 1942 by Harry Warren and Mack Gordon. It has become a jazz standard. John Ashbery was an American poet. He passed away on September 3, 2017. Walter Becker, the cofounder of the American rock band Steely Dan, also died on that date. "Peg" and "Deacon Blues" are two rock classics by that band. The Kunstkammer (cabinet of art) of Emperor Rudolf II (1552–1612) was one of the most diverse and impressive collections of its time. He purchased Albrecht Dürer's renowned altarpiece "The Feast of the Rose Garlands" (1506) in 1606 and had it transported across the continent from Venice to his castle in Prague. Dexter Gordon was an American jazz tenor saxophonist. He recorded "There Will Never Be Another You" in 1967. A jazz contrafact is a borrowed chord progression. In improvisation, it most often manifests as a new melody overlaid on a familiar harmonic structure. We might think of it as an improvised sample. Dexter Gordon, like most jazz players, frequently used the device of the contrafact in his solos. "All the Things You Are" is a song that is frequently used in this way. Gordon inserted this Jerome Kern tune into his 1946 recording of "Boston Bernie."

"America [April]" references very broadly Czesław Miłosz's poem "Dedication."

"Self-Portrait in Suspension" has as its epigraph perhaps Issa's most famous haiku, which he composed upon the death of his daughter. Khaled al-Asaad was chief of the UNESCO World Heritage Site in Palmyra, Syria. He was beheaded by the Islamic State of Iraq and Syria on August 18, 2015. He was 83 years old. His body was actually hung from a traffic light, his severed head placed below. During 2015, ISIS fighters intentionally destroyed antiquities and ancient buildings in Palmyra, including the Temple of Bel (also known as the Temple of Baal), which had been constructed in 32 CE. The *I-Ching* is an ancient Chinese divination text. My three pet mollies were named after the Pittsburgh Pirates pitcher Dock Ellis, who threw a no-hitter on June 12, 1970. He is said to have been high on LSD at the time, but I didn't know that when I named my fish. It just seemed that every pack of baseball cards I bought as a kid had a Dock Ellis card in it. This poem references *Common Wild Flowers*, a Penguin paperback by John Hutchinson, and *The Complete Book of Solitaire and Patience Games,* by Albert H. Morehead and Geoffrey Mott-Smith, which is published by Random House.

"Passage" is a poem I attempted to write in the style and tone of Matthew Zapruder. It contains a few bits of text sampled from his poems and is dedicated to him. I love his poems. It is also a poem that references the Cape May–Lewes Ferry. Go, little boat, go.

"A Short History of Sorrow" is dedicated to Sandy Tarant. It alludes to information found in *The Genius of Birds* by Jennifer Ackerman. Cessna and Piper refer to small aircraft. Sarin gas is a potentially deadly nerve agent the Syrian government has been repeatedly accused of using against its own population.

"Here, After" is dedicated to Larry Graber. The book referenced at the end of this poem is Jack Gilbert's *The Great Fires.* I like to believe, as Gilbert did, that it is inaccurate to say a marriage fails. It is truer to say that we came to the end of our triumph.

"Death Dream in August" opens with an epigraph from Amy Lowell's poem "A Gift." I will always be deeply indebted to Lowell for the remarkable traveling scholarship she established and from which I have benefited.

"Self-Portrait with Moon" references the expedition of Henry Worsley, who set out alone in 2015 at the age of 55 in an effort to become the first person to cross the Antarctic continent unsupported and unassisted. Mark Synnott's article, "This Man Will Spend 80 Days Walking Antarctica Alone," was published in the *National Geographic* of November 9, 2015 (https://news.national geographic.com/2015/11/151109-south-pole-antarctic-explorers-shackleton -expedition/).

On January 22nd, after seventy-one days, having covered nearly eight hundred nautical miles, Worsley called and arranged to be airlifted out. He died days later in a hospital in Punta Arenas, Chile, from complications from septic shock and bacterial peritonitis. The event is described at length in David Grann's "The White Darkness: A Solitary Journey across Antarctica," in *The New Yorker*, February 12 and 19, 2018 (https://www.newyorker.com /maga zine/2018/02/12/the-white-darkness).

"America [emptiness]" has an epigraph from a *Los Angeles Times* article posted on September 3, 2013 (http://www.latimes.com/science/sciencenow/la-sci-sn -frog-earless-hear-sound-mouth-listen-20130903-story.html). The Gardiner's frog lives in the Seychelles. On September 2, 2013, Diana Nyad became the first person to swim from Cuba to Florida without the protection of a shark cage. The journey took 53 hours.

"Greetings from Richmond" alludes to Bishop's amazing poem "At the Fish-houses." *Shen* is a term used in traditional Chinese medicine for spirit or psyche.

"Postscript from the Heterochronic-Archipelagic Now" takes its ridiculously wonky (tongue in cheek) title from concepts and language found in the essay "Notes on Metamodernism," by Timotheus Vermeulen and Robin van den Akker. It appeared in 2010 in the *Journal of Aesthetics & Culture,* 2:1 (DOI: 10.3402/jac.v2i0.5677). There is a lot of conflicting advice about how best to care for indoor gardenias, which are notoriously fussy. What works for mine may not work for yours. There are many "Words of the Year" determined and announced annually by various organizations. The American Dialect Society's list is the oldest in the English language. Other sources include Oxford University Press, which offers an annual language report, and Merriam-Webster, which also lists its own Words of the Year. Oxford's recent words have included *post-truth, emoji,* and *selfie.* The American Dialect Society has recently listed *fake news, dumpster fire,* the singular *they,* and *hashtag. Refudiate* was

Oxford's rather (delightfully?) snarky 2010 word of the year; the word was "coined" by Sarah Palin and seems to have come from a merging of the words *refuse* and *repudiate*. *Simulacrum* has never been, as far as I know, the word of the year anywhere. *Known-knowns* and *unknown-unknowns* will be remembered as two of the phrases use by then Secretary of Defense Donald Rumsfeld in 2002 in his response to questions about the lack of evidence linking Iraq to terrorism and weapons of mass destruction. President Donald Trump's attorney Rudolph Giuliani offered that "Truth isn't truth" in an interview with Chuck Todd on *Meet the Press* on August 19, 2018. MRI scans have shown that an eight-week course in mindfulness training appears to reduce the size of the amygdala, the region of the brain associated with stress, fear, and emotion. As this primal region shrinks, the prefrontal cortex, associated with awareness and higher order brain functions, such as decision-making, appears to become denser. Peggy Noonan's opinion piece in *The Wall Street Journal* on April 26, 2018, carried this headline: "What Does This Moment Demand of Us?"

"A Rhetoric" was written in direct response to my experiences serving on an academic search committee for a colleague in the area of rhetoric and composition. The job advertisement intentionally cast a large net, and I was genuinely shocked by the wide varieties of research projects that the many, many, many interesting and able candidates were conducting. Who knew there were so many modes of rhetoric, or that everything might be seen in some way as rhetorical?

There was a shutdown of the United States federal government that began at midnight EST on Saturday, January 20, 2018, and ended on the evening of Monday, January 22. The United Kingdom appointed a Minister of Loneliness to combat what Prime Minister Theresa May called the "sad reality of modern life." According to their government figures, more than 9 million people in the UK "always or often feel lonely" and "around 200,000 older people have not had a conversation with a friend or relative in more than a month," according to an *NPR* article published on January 17, 2018. "This Land Is Your Land" is one of the most famous traditional American songs. Its lyrics were written over a preexisting melody by Woody Guthrie in 1940. According to a CNN report on November 24, 2017: "A woman walking her dogs near her western New York home was fatally shot Wednesday by a man who told police he mistook her for a deer. Rosemary Billquist, 43, was hit by a bullet from a single-shot pistol fired by neighbor Thomas B. Jadlowski, said Sgt. Josh Ostrander of the Chautauqua County Sheriff's Office." After first releasing his dog so that she would be spared carbon monoxide poisoning, my neighbor did, in fact, commit suicide, as described in this poem.